Beginner's Book of BBQ

Easy Recipes for Your Next BBQ Party

Copyright Material

Sign-up Now
and Be Notified of New Books

Website: readbooks.today

Table of Contents

Rubs

Classic BBQ Rub

Prep Time: 5 minutes
Cooking Time: 5 minutes
Servings: 1 cup

Ingredients

- 1 ½ tablespoons paprika
- 3 tablespoons turbinado sugar
- 1 tablespoon each of dry mustard, chili powder, black pepper, granulated garlic & granulated onion
- 2 tablespoons kosher salt

Directions

1. Combine the entire ingredients together in a medium-sized mixing bowl; mix well & store in an airtight container until ready to use.

Texas BBQ Rub

Prep Time: 5 minutes
Cooking Time: 5 minutes
Servings: 4 persons

Ingredients

- 1 tablespoon smoked paprika
- ¼ cup light brown sugar
- 1 teaspoon each of ground cayenne pepper, chili powder, onion powder, garlic powder & salt
- ½ teaspoon ground black pepper

Directions

1. Combine the entire ingredients together in a medium-sized mixing bowl; mix well. Ensure that the brown sugar is completely broken up.
2. Store in an airtight container until ready to use.

Montreal Rub

Prep Time: 5 minutes
Cooking Time: 5 minutes
Servings: ½ cup

Ingredients

- 2 tablespoons black peppercorns
- 1 tablespoon plus 1 teaspoon coarse kosher salt
- 1 teaspoon coriander seeds
- 2 teaspoons dill seeds
- 1 tablespoon mustard seeds
- 1 teaspoon red chili pepper flakes, crushed
- 1 tablespoon plus 1 teaspoon dried garlic, minced

Directions

1. Over medium heat in a small skillet; cook the mustard seeds with peppercorns, coriander seeds, and dill seeds for a minute or two, until fragrant & starting to pop, stirring the ingredients frequently. Transfer the mixture to a mortar and pestle; coarsely crush. Add chili flakes, garlic, crush, and salt; mix well.

Kansas City Rub

Prep Time: 5 minutes
Cooking Time: 5 minutes
Servings: ⅔ cup

Ingredients

- 2 teaspoons fresh ground black pepper
- 1 teaspoon ground cayenne pepper
- 2 tablespoons ground paprika
- 1 tablespoon each of white sugar, garlic salt, chili powder & celery salt
- ½ teaspoon dry mustard
- 2 tablespoons brown sugar

Directions

1. Combine the entire ingredients together in a medium-sized mixing bowl; mix well. Store in an airtight, sealed container until ready to use.

Southwestern Rub

Prep Time: 5 minutes
Cooking Time: 5 minutes
Servings: 2 cups

Ingredients

- 3 teaspoons chili powder
- 1 teaspoon each of ground coriander, cumin, granulated garlic, cayenne, cracked black pepper & kosher salt
- 2 teaspoons paprika

Directions

1. Combine the entire ingredients together in an airtight container; shake the ingredients well & use it up.

Jamaican Jerk Rub

Prep Time: 5 minutes
Cooking Time: 5 minutes
Servings: 3 tablespoons

Ingredients

- 1 ½ teaspoons ground allspice
- 1 teaspoon curry powder
- ⅛ teaspoon ground cloves
- 1 ½ teaspoons paprika
- ¼ teaspoon each of grated nutmeg & ground cinnamon
- 1 ½ teaspoons cayenne pepper
- ¾ teaspoon black pepper
- 1 ½ teaspoons thyme, dried
- 1 teaspoon sugar
- ½ teaspoon salt

Directions

1. Thoroughly combine the entire all spices together & store the mix in an airtight container.
2. To use, rub on shrimp, pork, or chicken a minimum of 15 to 20 minutes before you plan to grill. Enough for 3 pounds of meat.

BBQ Sauces

Dr Pepper BBQ Sauce

Prep Time: 5 minutes
Cooking Time: 10 minutes
Servings: 32 persons

Ingredients

- 1 cup brown sugar
- 12 ounces Dr. Pepper
- 1 teaspoon coarse salt
- 2 cups ketchup
- 1 teaspoon chili powder
- ½ teaspoon liquid smoke
- 1 tablespoon Worcestershire Sauce
- ½ teaspoon granulated garlic

Directions

1. Add the entire ingredients together into a large-sized saucepan; whisk until combined well.
2. Place it over moderate heat & cook until mixture just starts to bubble, stirring every now and then.
3. Decrease the heat & let simmer until the sugar is completely dissolved, for 5 minutes, stirring often.
4. Store in a refrigerator in an airtight container until ready to use.

Sweet & Spicy BBQ Sauce

Prep Time: 5 minutes
Cooking Time: 40 minutes
Servings: 5 cups

Ingredients

- 1 jalapeño pepper, seeded & minced
- 2 garlic cloves, minced
- 1 tablespoon Worcestershire sauce
- ½ cup sweet onion, chopped
- 1 teaspoon celery seeds
- 1 cup apple cider vinegar
- ½ cup apple juice
- 1 teaspoon freshly ground black pepper
- ½ cup honey
- 1 teaspoon kosher salt
- 1 bottle Heinz ketchup (32-ounces)
- 1 tablespoon olive oil
- ½ teaspoon dried red pepper, crushed
- 1 cup dark brown sugar, firmly packed

Directions

1. Over medium-high heat in a large saucepan; heat up the olive oil until hot. Once done; sauté the onion with jalapeño pepper & minced garlic until tender, for 3 to 5 minutes.
2. Stir in the vinegar, Worcestershire sauce, dark brown sugar, apple juice, ketchup, honey, celery seeds, freshly ground black pepper, dried crushed red pepper & kosher salt. Bring the mixture to a boil, stirring every now and then. Decrease the heat to low & let simmer for half an hour, stirring every now and then. Use immediately or refrigerate up to 1 month in an airtight container.

North Carolina BBQ Sauce

Prep Time: 5 minutes
Cooking Time: 5 minutes
Servings: 2 cups

Ingredients

- 1 tablespoon cayenne pepper
- 1 cup white vinegar
- 1 tablespoon brown sugar
- 1 cup cider vinegar
- 1 teaspoon ground black pepper
- 1 tablespoon hot pepper sauce or to taste
- 1 teaspoon salt

Directions

1. Combine cider vinegar with hot pepper sauce, white vinegar, cayenne pepper, brown sugar, pepper and salt in a bottle or jar with a lid. Refrigerate for a day or two before using; shaking the jar every now and then. Store in a refrigerator for up to 2 months.

Texas Style BBQ Sauce

Prep Time: 5 minutes
Cooking Time: 25 minutes
Servings: 1 ¾ cups

Ingredients

- 1 cup ketchup
- 2 garlic cloves, minced
- 1 small onion, chopped
- ¼ cup brown sugar, packed
- 1 tablespoon yellow mustard
- 2 tablespoons apple cider vinegar
- ¼ cup lemon juice, fresh
- 1 tablespoon butter
- 2 teaspoons chili powder
- 1 tablespoon Worcestershire sauce
- 2 tablespoons tomato paste

Directions

1. Over medium heat in a large-sized saucepan; heat up the butter until melted. Once done; add & cook the onion until tender, for 2 to 3 minutes, stirring frequently.
2. Add & cook the garlic for a minute more. Stir in the leftover ingredients; bring the mixture to a boil, over moderate heat. Decrease the heat & let simmer until the flavors are blended well, for 17 to 20 minutes, uncovered.

Hoisin BBQ Sauce

Prep Time: 10 minutes
Cooking Time: 20 minutes
Servings: 4 persons

Ingredients

- 2 garlic cloves, minced
- ½ teaspoon sesame oil
- 2 tablespoons each of dry sherry & rice vinegar
- ⅓ cup water.
- 1 tablespoon each of ketchup & soy sauce
- Olive oil
- 1 scallion, chopped
- ½ cup hoisin sauce

Directions

1. Cook the garlic cloves with olive oil in a saucepan & cook for a minute. Stir in ½ cup of hoisin sauce followed by dry sherry and rice vinegar, ketchup, and soy sauce and ⅓ cup of water.
2. Let simmer for 17 to 20 minutes, until thickened, stirring frequently. Let cool and then, add in the chopped scallion & sesame oil.

Memphis BBQ Sauce

Prep Time: 10 minutes
Cooking Time: 35 minutes
Servings: 3 cups

Ingredients

- ½ cup brown sugar
- 2 cups ketchup
- ¼ cup cider vinegar
- 1 tablespoon onion powder
- ½ teaspoon celery seed
- 2 teaspoons garlic powder
- ½ cup prepared yellow mustard
- 2 teaspoons liquid smoke
- 1 tablespoon chili powder
- 3 tablespoons Worcestershire sauce
- 1 tablespoon ground black pepper
- 2 tablespoons canola oil
- ½ teaspoon cayenne pepper
- 1 teaspoon salt

Directions

1. Combine the entire ingredients (except oil) together in a large-sized saucepan, over moderate heat.
2. Bring the mixture to a low boil, stirring every now and then.
3. Decrease the heat & let simmer for 20 to 25 minutes, stirring every now and then.
4. Remove from heat & whisk in the oil until blended well.
5. Store in a refrigerator in an air-tight container.

Appetizers

Peach & Prosciutto Skewers

Prep Time: 10 minutes
Cooking Time: 10 minutes
Servings: 15 persons

Ingredients

- 100 grams prosciutto, sliced very thinly (approximately 0.22 pound)
- 3 peaches medium-large
- Balsamic reduction, for drizzling

Directions

1. Preheat your grill over medium high heat.
2. Prepare Prosciutto and Peaches: Slice the peaches into 1 to 1 ½" thick wedges; ensure that you don't remove the skin. Slice the prosciutto into 4" long x 1" wide strips. Wrap a strip of prosciutto around a wedge of peach and then thread onto a metal skewer. Repeat until you have utilized all the peaches.
3. To Grill: To prevent sticking; lightly coat the peaches threaded on skewers with olive oil. Grill the skewers until char marks start to appear, for a few minutes per side.
4. To Serve: Remove the peach prosciutto appetizers. Place on a large-sized serving platter. Just before serving, don't forget to drizzle the appetizers and platter with balsamic reduction. Place a toothpick in each appetizer. Serve warm and enjoy.

Prosciutto Wrapped Asparagus

Prep Time: 10 minutes
Cooking Time: 10 minutes
Servings: 4 persons

Ingredients

- 16 large asparagus spears (approximately ¾" to 1" at base); trim the tough ends
- 2 tablespoons olive oil
- 16 slices of prosciutto, thinly sliced
- Pepper & salt to taste

Directions

1. Prepare the gas or charcoal grill for medium-to-medium high direct cooking.
2. Trim the tough end from the asparagus spears; thoroughly wash & pat them dry using a paper towel.
3. Wrap each spear with a prosciutto slice.
4. Brush the wrapped spears with some olive oil.
5. Lightly season with pepper & salt to taste.
6. Place the spears over prepared grill & cook until the asparagus has some slight chars & prosciutto is crisp, turning as required to evenly cook all sides. Ensure that the asparagus must be tender but still firm.

Tequila Lime Chargrilled Oysters

Prep Time: 40 minutes
Cooking Time: 10 minutes
Servings: 6 persons

Ingredients

- ½ pound jumbo lump crab meat
- 2 dozen shucked oysters, in the shell

For Cilantro, Tequila & Lime Compound Butter:
- 1 shallot, minced
- ¾ pound unsalted butter, softened
- 1 tablespoon lime juice, fresh
- 2 serrano peppers; seeded & minced
- 1 tablespoon cilantro, finely chopped
- 1 teaspoon lime zest
- 2 teaspoon silver tequila
- 1 garlic clove, fresh, minced
- 1 teaspoon each of pepper & salt

For Breadcrumb Cheese Topping:
- 2 tablespoons creole seasoning
- 1 ½ cup panko breadcrumbs
- ¾ cup Fontina cheese, finely shredded

Directions

1. For Compound Butter: Fold the entire Compound Butter ingredients together using a rubber spatula in a large-sized mixing bowl; until completely incorporated.
2. Once done, lay out on approximately 2 ft. of plastic wrap.
3. Spoon the prepared butter mixture in the middle of the plastic wrap & roll it into a log.
4. Twist the ends of plastic wrap to seal & place in a refrigerator until hard.
5. For Chargrilled Oysters: Preheat your grill over high heat.
6. Once the oysters have been shucked, make sure to scrape the muscle from the shell so that the oysters will easily slide off the shell.
7. With your oysters on the half shell spread out, top them in this order: a pinch of the breadcrumb mixture followed by ¼" thick slice of compound butter, lump crab meat & lastly a pinch of the breadcrumb mixture.
8. Grill until the breadcrumbs have browned and butter has melted, for 3 to 5 minutes, over high heat. Serve immediately with some crostini bread & enjoy.

Fig Crostini

Prep Time: 20 minutes
Cooking Time: 20 minutes
Servings: 12 persons

Ingredients

- 12 figs, cut lengthwise into half
- ¼ cup pistachios, chopped, toasted
- 1 cup mascarpone
- ⅓ cup Renée's Balsamic Vinaigrette
- 24 baguette slices (approximately ½" thick)
- ¼ cup honey, divided

Directions

1. Heat your barbecue over medium heat.
2. Toss the figs with vinaigrette & let stand for 8 to 10 minutes. In the meantime, combine the cheese with 3 tablespoons of honey until blended well.
3. Grill the figs until softened slightly, for a minute or two, cut sides down. Remove from the barbecue; set aside. Add bread to the barbecue & grill until grill-marked on both sides & toasted, for a minute or two per side.
4. Cut the figs crosswise into half & spread the toasted slices with cream cheese mixture; top with figs, leftover honey & nuts.

Spicy Buffalo Wings

Prep Time: 10 minutes
Cooking Time: 30 minutes
Servings: 6 persons

Ingredients

For Wings:

- 3 pounds chicken wings (cut into sections, if whole; discarding the wing tips or reserve it for the stock)
- Vegetable oil, as required, for grill
- 1 ½ teaspoons kosher salt
- ½ teaspoon black pepper

For Buffalo Sauce:

- ¼ cup plus 2 tablespoons red hot cayenne pepper sauce
- 6 tablespoons unsalted butter
- ½ teaspoon onion powder
- 1 garlic clove, minced
- ¾ teaspoon sugar
- ½ teaspoon chili powder
- ¼ teaspoon kosher salt

Directions

1. Preheat your grill over medium-high heat. Season the wings with pepper & salt.
2. Dip a wad of paper towels in oil using grill tongs and then, rub the grill grate carefully until glossy & coated.
3. Grill the coated wings for 17 to 20 minutes, until turn golden brown, crispy & cooked through, covered, flipping every now and then. Keep an eye on the hot grill: if the wings begin to burn or there are flare-ups, immediately reduce the heat or move the wings to a cooler part of the grill. The wings just have a nice & even golden-brown color and don't have the grill marks on them.
4. Meanwhile, prepare the sauce. Combine the garlic and butter in a microwave-safe bowl. Cook in the microwave for a minute, until the butter is completely melted. Stir in the onion powder, hot sauce, chili powder, sugar & salt.
5. Dip the cooked wings into the prepared sauce; serve immediately.

Side Dishes

Mexican Corn on the Cob

Prep Time: 15 minutes
Cooking Time: 15 minutes
Servings: 8 persons

Ingredients

- 8 ears corn on the cob, husked
- ½ cup mayonnaise
- 1 tablespoon ground ancho chile pepper
- ½ cup Cotija cheese, freshly grated
- Juice of 1 lime, fresh
- ¼ cup butter, melted, or as required
- 1 teaspoon smoked paprika
- A pinch of salt, or to taste
- 1 lime, sliced

Directions

1. Lightly oil the grate of an outdoor grill and then, preheat it over high heat.
2. Combine lime juice with mayonnaise, smoked paprika, and ancho chile powder in a large bowl; whisk the ingredients until completely smooth. Refrigerate until required.
3. Fill a large pot with salted water and bring it to a boil, over moderate heat. Boil the corn for 5 minutes in the salted water. Once done; drain the corn well.
4. Place the ears of corn over the hot grill & cook for a couple of minutes, until the kernels start to turn brown & caramelize. Turn the corn over & continue cooking the other side until browned with charred slightly, caramelized spots, turning the ears after minute or two.
5. Brush the corn generously with the melted butter & ancho-lime mayonnaise until the kernels are nicely coated. Sprinkle the ears with Cotija cheese & salt. Garnish with the lime slices. Serve and enjoy.

BBQ Baked Beans

Prep Time: 10 minutes
Cooking Time: 50 minutes
Servings: 8 persons

Ingredients

- 1 tablespoon olive oil
- 1 red bell pepper, chopped
- 1/2 onion, chopped
- 2 cloves garlic, chopped
- 2 (28-ounce) cans baked beans
- 1/2 cup brown sugar
- ⅓ cup BBQ seasoning, recipe follows
- ¼ cup molasses
- 1 cup BBQ sauce, recipe follows
- ¾ cup chopped pork or beef brisket

For BBQ Seasoning:
- 1 1/2 cups paprika
- ¾ cup sugar
- 3 ¾ tablespoons onion powder

For BBQ Sauce:
- ½ cup apple cider vinegar
- 2 cups ketchup
- ½ tablespoon onion powder
- 5 tablespoons light brown sugar
- 1 tablespoon Worcestershire sauce
- ½ tablespoon black pepper, fresh ground
- 5 tablespoons sugar
- 1 tablespoon lemon juice, fresh
- ½ tablespoon ground mustard
- 1 cup water

Directions

1. Preheat your oven to 275F.
2. Over medium heat in a large Dutch oven; heat up the oil until hot. Once done; sauté the red pepper, garlic, and onion for 2 minutes, until softened. Add the baked beans & leftover ingredients; bring the mixture to a low simmer. Cover the beans & bake for 40 to 45 minutes.

For BBQ Seasoning:

1. Add the entire ingredients together into a large-sized mixing bowl; give it a good stir until combined well. Keep for up to 6 months in an airtight container.

For BBQ Sauce:

1. Combine the entire ingredients together in a large saucepan; bring mixture to a boil, over moderate heat. Once done; decrease the heat to a simmer. Cook for 1 hour & 15 minutes, uncovered, stirring every now and then.

Grilled Sweet Potatoes with Lemon-Herb Sauce

Prep Time: 10 minutes
Cooking Time: 20 minutes
Servings: 6 persons

Ingredients

- 2 pounds sweet potatoes, scrubbed well & sliced into ¼" thick rounds
- ½ red onion, small, chopped finely
- 2 teaspoon lemon zest, grated plus ¼ cup lemon juice
- ¼ cup fresh mint, chopped
- 3 tablespoons olive oil, divided, plus more for serving
- 1 small Fresno chili, seeded & chopped finely
- 2 tablespoons hemp seed, optional
- Pepper & kosher salt as required

For Serving:
- Greek plain yogurt

Directions

1. Preheat your grill over medium heat. Combine the onion with lemon juice in a small-sized mixing bowl. Let sit; ensure that you toss it every now and then.
2. Toss the sweet potatoes with approximately 2 tablespoons of oil & ¼ teaspoon each of pepper and salt in a large bowl. Grill for a couple of minutes on each side, until charred slightly & tender.
3. Stir leftover oil with chile, lemon zest & hemp into the bowl with onions and then, stir in the fresh mint. You should be getting approximately ½ cup of relish.
4. Spread the Greek yogurt onto a large platter & drizzle with some oil. Arrange the sweet potatoes on top of the yogurt & spoon the mint relish over the pieces. Serve and enjoy.

Cowboy Caviar

Prep Time: 15 minutes
Cooking Time: 10 minutes
Servings: 12 persons

Ingredients

- 1 can blackeye beans, rinsed & drained
- ½ cup grilled bell peppers, diced
- 1 can black bean, rinsed & drained
- ½ cup fresh cilantro, chopped
- 1 cup sweet corn, grilled
- ¾ cup zesty Italian dressing
- 1 cup tomatoes, grilled & diced
- ½ cup grilled onions, diced
- 1 avocado, diced
- ½ teaspoon garlic salt
- Olive oil, black pepper & sea salt for grilling

Directions

1. Arrange the sliced onion, tomatoes & bell peppers in a grilling basket. Brush the ears of sweet corn & the veggies in the basket with some olive oil & then, sprinkle with black pepper and sea salt. Grill until grill marks start to appear, for 4 to 6 minutes per side, over medium high heat, turning every now and then.
2. Let the veggies to cool down and then, dice the grilled tomatoes, onions, and peppers. Cut the grilled sweet corn from the cob.
3. Put the rinsed & drained blackeye peas and black beans into a large bowl. Add the onions, avocado, peppers, tomatoes, zesty Italian dressing, cilantro & garlic salt; give the ingredients a good stir until combined well.
4. Store in a refrigerator until ready to serve.

Corn Pudding

Prep Time: 5 minutes
Cooking Time: 10 minutes
Servings: 8 persons

Ingredients

- 3 eggs, large, separated
- 1 cup heavy whipping cream
- 6 ears of sweet corn, shucked
- 1 to 3 teaspoons sugar
- ¼ teaspoon nutmeg, freshly grated, or to taste
- Olive oil
- ½ teaspoon cream of tartar
- Freshly ground black pepper & salt (kosher or coarse or sea), as required

Directions

1. Set up your grill grate for direct grilling & preheat it over high heat.
2. Brush each ear of corn lightly with some olive oil then, season with pepper and salt.
3. Next, place the coated corn carefully on the grate; grill for 2 to 3 minutes on each side, until all sides turn golden brown; turning as required, using a pair of tongs. Transfer to a clean, large cutting board & let cool until easy to handle.
4. Remove the corn kernels from the cobs, using lengthwise strokes of a chef's knife. Break 3 of the cobs into half & place them over medium heat in a saucepan with the cream; bring it to a simmer. Gently simmer the cream for 12 to 15 minutes. Remove the pan from heat & let the cream to cool down.
5. Next, puree half of the corn kernels in a food processor until you get smooth paste like consistency. Add in the egg yolks; process on high power until mixed well. Strain in the cooled cream; pulse until just mixed. Transfer the prepared mixture to a large-sized mixing bowl & stir in the nutmeg and leftover whole corn kernels. Season with pepper and salt to taste. Taste for seasoning and feel free to add more of nutmeg and/or sugar as required.
6. Set up your grill for indirect grilling & preheat it to medium heat.
7. Beat the cream of tartar with egg whites in a clean metal bowl (using either a hand mixer or a stand mixer) until soft peaks form. Gently fold the prepared egg whites into the pureed corn mixture using a large, rubber spatula. Oil the baking dish lightly and then, spoon the corn mixture into it. Ensure that you don't over fold.
8. Place the filled baking dish (away from the heat) in middle of the hot grate; cover the grill & cook for 20 to 30 minutes, until the pudding is browned on top, puffed & cooked through. Serve immediately & enjoy.

Buffalo Mac N' Cheese

Prep Time: 10 minutes
Cooking Time: 40 minutes
Servings: 20 persons

Ingredients

- ½ cup bacon bits
- 1 pkg elbow macaroni (16-ounces)
- ¼ cup butter

For Cheese Sauce

- 8 ounces mild cheddar cheese (approximately 2 cups), shredded
- ¼ cup flour
- 4 ounces 4 cheese blend (approximately 1 cup)
- 1 pkg cream cheese
- 8 ounces sharp cheddar cheese (approximately 2 cups), shredded
- 3 cups whole milk
- ½ cup Moore's Marinade Buffalo Wing Sauce
- 4 ounces Parmesan cheese (approximately 1 cup), shredded
- 2 teaspoon each of black pepper & salt

Directions

1. Boil pasta according to instructions on pkg with some salt (6-7 min), then set aside in large mixing bowl

For Cheese Sauce:
1. Over medium low heat in a saucepan; heat the butter until melted.
2. Once done; slowly whisk in the flour and cook until it thickens, for a minute or two.
3. Next, slowly whisk in the milk; bring the mixture to a slow boil.
4. Fold in the cream cheese; once the mixture begins to thicken.
5. Continue to whisk the ingredients slowly until sauce is smooth and cream cheese is completely melted
6. Add Buffalo Wing Sauce, pepper, and salt; continue to whisk until the mixture is evenly colored and smooth.

For Combine Cheeses:
1. Add the entire cheeses (set 1 cup of the sharp cheddar cheese aside) in a large-sized mixing bowl
2. Stir in cheese with cheese sauce and pasta.
3. When blended well, place into a small-sized aluminum half pan
4. Add the bacon bits and leftover cup of the sharp cheddar cheese on top

To Cook:
1. Place into smoker and cook until the cheese on the top is completely melted, for 35 to 40 minutes at 250 F. Ensure that you don't over-smoke the ingredients.

Side Dishes

BBQ Cole Slaw

Prep Time: 10 minutes
Cooking Time: 10 minutes
Servings: 8 persons

Ingredients

- 2 bags coleslaw mix (16-ounces each)
- ⅓ cup ketchup
- 1 tablespoon Worcestershire sauce
- ¼ cup white vinegar
- 1 tablespoon dried onion flakes, minced
- ⅓ cup sugar
- 2 teaspoon salt, or to taste
- ½ cup canola or vegetable oil

Directions

1. Place the coleslaw mix in a large-sized mixing bowl.
2. Next, over moderate heat in a large saucepan; combine ketchup with oil, sugar, vinegar, Worcestershire sauce, onion & salt. Cook until the sugar is just dissolved. Remove from the heat; set aside and let cool until easy to handle.
3. Pour the cooled dressing on top of the coleslaw mix. Gently toss the ingredients to coat.
4. Before serving; don't forget to refrigerate it for 4 to 6 hours.

Greek Salad

Prep Time: 20 minutes
Cooking Time: 20 minutes
Servings: 4 persons

Ingredients

- 1 slab sheep's milk feta cheese (6 ounce), 1" thick
- 4 hearts romaine, bottoms trimmed, cut lengthwise into half
- 1 red onion, small, cut into ¼" thick rounds
- 8 to 10 vegetarian stuffed grape leaves; fresh or canned
- ¼ cup Kalamata olives
- Red wine vinegar
- 2 to 3 small Persian or Kirby cucumbers, cut into 1" pieces
- Sea salt
- 1 ripe, medium, heirloom tomato, cored & cut into 1" chunks
- Extra-virgin olive oil
- 1 teaspoon oregano, dried
- Freshly ground black pepper & kosher salt to taste

Optional Ingredients:
- Pepperoncini
- 4 to 5 anchovy fillets, oil-packed
- Melba toast or Breadsticks

Directions

1. Heat a charcoal fire in advance (ensure that the coals turn white).
2. In the meantime, brush the onion rounds and romaine with some oil & season with the oregano, pepper & kosher salt. Place the olives and feta on a rectangular piece of aluminum foil; create a shallow boat by folding the edges upward and then, drizzle them with the oil as well.
3. Lightly coat the grill grate with some vegetable oil or cooking spray.
4. Place the stuffed grape leaves, onion, romaine & olive/feta packet over the hot grill; cook for 3 to 5 minutes, until all sides of the vegetables show some nice light charred spots. Using a pair of tongs; carefully remove from the grill grate.
5. Make a bed of the grilled romaine (try keeping the halves as it is) on a large serve platter & top with the cucumbers, tomato, olives, grilled stuffed grape leaves & onion. Cut the feta into 1" cubes; toss them over the top. Generously drizzle the whole thing with some oil and lightly season with black pepper and sea salt to taste.
6. Top with the pepperoncini and anchovies. Serve with oil and red wine vinegar with some Melba toast or breadsticks on side. Enjoy.

Firecracker Potato Salad

Prep Time: 20 minutes
Cooking Time: 20 minutes
Servings: 16 persons

Ingredients

- 30 red potatoes (approximately 3 pounds), small, quartered
- 1 teaspoon salt
- 2 tablespoons olive oil
- ½ teaspoon pepper

For Dressing:
- ½ cup onion, finely chopped
- 1 ½ cups mayonnaise
- ¼ cup Dijon mustard
- 2 tablespoons sweet pickle relish
- ¼ teaspoon cayenne pepper
- ½ teaspoon paprika

For Salad:
- 2 celery ribs, chopped finely
- 6 large eggs, hard-boiled, chopped
- Fresh chives, minced, optional

Directions

1. Toss the potatoes with oil, pepper, and salt; place in a grill basket or wok. Grill until the potatoes are fork-tender, for 20 to 25 minutes, over medium heat, covered, stirring every now and then. Transfer the cooked potatoes to a large-sized mixing bowl; set aside & let cool.

2. Combine the entire dressing ingredients together in a small-sized mixing bowl. Add the eggs, celery, and dressing to the potatoes; gently toss to combine. Cover & refrigerate until cold, for an hour or two. Just before serving; sprinkle with minced chives. Enjoy.

Main Dishes

Grilled Rib Eye with Romaine Marmalade and Watercress

Prep Time: 20 minutes
Cooking Time: 40 minutes
Servings: 6 persons

Ingredients

For Steak:
- 1 bone-in rib eye chop (24 ounce), approximately 2 ½" thick
- Cracked pepper
- Large grain sea salt
- French butter
- Extra virgin olive oil

For Romaine Marmalade & Watercress:
- 4 bunches of watercress (approximately 2 cups of leaves), organic, stems removed
- 1 garlic clove, small
- 2 whole romaine lettuce leaves
- Juice of 1 lemon, fresh
- ¼ bunch each of flat-leaf parsley & cilantro, fresh & trimmed
- 2 tablespoons extra-virgin olive oil
- Freshly ground pepper & fine sea salt, to taste

Directions

1. For Steak: Generously sprinkle the steak with olive oil, pepper, and salt; ensure that the steak is completely covered. Lightly wrap & place for overnight in a refrigerator.
2. An hour before you plan to cook the steak; remove the steak from your refrigerator; set aside at room temperature and then, preheat your grill (ensure that the embers should be glowing and burned down, without any flames) in advance.
3. When ready, place the coated steak carefully on the middle of hot grill & cook for 10 minutes; rotate right and left until you get nice grill marks on both sides. When done, remove the steak to the coolest part of grill & cook for 25 to 30 more minutes. When done, place the cooked steak on a rack set inside a sheet pan. Add a knob of French butter over it & tent it lightly with tin foil; let rest for 15 more minutes.

For Romaine Marmalade & Watercress:
1. Combine watercress with garlic, romaine, parsley, cilantro, lemon juice, pepper and salt in a food processor or blender. Add oil & puree until completely smooth; set aside.

To Serve:
1. Slice each steak evenly into 3 thick portions. Spoon same portions of the prepared watercress-romaine puree over the plates. Arrange the sliced steak on each plate. Strain the steak pan juices & pour them over the meat.

Grilled Mongolian Pork Chops

Prep Time: 20 minutes
Cooking Time: 40 minutes
Servings: 2 persons

Ingredients

- 2 thick center cut bone-in pork chops (10 ounce each)
- 1 tablespoon fresh ginger, grated
- 4 garlic cloves, minced
- 1 tablespoon rice vinegar
- ½ cup hoisin sauce
- 1 ½ tablespoons soy sauce
- 1 tablespoon red wine vinegar
- 2 teaspoons sesame oil
- 1 tablespoon sherry vinegar
- ½ teaspoon freshly ground black pepper
- 2 teaspoons white sugar
- ½ teaspoon ground white pepper
- 1 ½ teaspoons hot sauce
- 3 tablespoons white sugar
- ¼ cup red wine vinegar
- 1 large egg yolk
- 2 tablespoons hot mustard powder
- ⅓ cup creme fraiche
- 1 teaspoon Dijon mustard
- ¼ teaspoon ground turmeric
- A pinch of cayenne pepper or to taste

Directions

1. Combine the hoisin sauce with soy sauce, garlic, ginger, 1 tablespoon of red wine vinegar, sesame oil, sherry vinegar, rice vinegar, 2 teaspoons of sugar, white pepper, hot sauce & black pepper in a large-sized mixing bowl. Thoroughly whisk the ingredients & set the mixture aside.
2. Place the pork chops in a large, resealable freezer bag; slightly pour more than ½ of the marinade into the freezer bag on top of the pork chops. Seal & refrigerate for overnight. Reserve the leftover marinade.
3. Next, combine egg yolk with 2 tablespoons hot mustard powder, 3 tablespoons sugar, and ¼ cup of red wine vinegar over medium-low heat in a small saucepan. Whisk the ingredients for 3 to 5 minutes, until thickened slightly; remove from the heat.
4. Stir in the Dijon mustard, creme fraiche, cayenne pepper, and turmeric. Refrigerate until required.
5. Remove the pork chops from marinade & using paper towels; pat them dry.
6. Preheat an outdoor grill over high heat & coat the grate lightly with oil.
7. Cook the pork chops for 3 to 4 minutes on each side, until browned & grill marks start to appear.
8. Move the pork chops directly above the heat source. Continue to cook over indirect medium heat for 20 to 25 more minutes, until no longer pink inside, brushing each side with the leftover marinade. Serve hot topped with the mustard sauce & enjoy.

Grilled Brown Sugar Pork Chops

Prep Time: 20 minutes
Cooking Time: 20 minutes
Servings: 6 persons

Ingredients

- 4 ounces boneless pork chops; 6 raw chops with refuse, 113 g
- ½ teaspoon ground ginger
- 4 tablespoons vegetable oil
- ½ cup apple juice
- 1 tablespoon soy sauce
- ½ cup firmly packed brown sugar
- 2 teaspoons cornstarch
- ½ cup water
- Pepper & salt to taste

Directions

1. Preheat an outdoor grill over high heat in advance.
2. Combine brown sugar with oil, apple juice, ginger, soy sauce, pepper & salt over moderate heat in a small saucepan. Bring the mixture to a boil. Combine cornstarch with water in a small bowl; whisk into the prepared brown sugar mixture. Giving the ingredients a good stir until thickened.
3. Before placing the pork chops over the grill; brush the grate lightly with some oil. Cook for 10 to 12 minutes, over hot coals, turning once during the cooking process. Just before you remove the chops from hot grill; don't forget to brush them with the sauce. Serve with the leftover sauce. Enjoy.

Spicy BBQ Pork Loin

Prep Time: 6 hours
Cooking Time: 1 hour & 30 minutes
Servings: 10 persons

Ingredients

For Pork:

- 2 ½ to 3pounds pork loin roast, center-cut, or pork tenderloin
- ½ teaspoon pepper
- 1tablespoon kosher salt

For Marinade:

- 2 tablespoons olive oil
- 4 tablespoons balsamic vinegar
- 2 tablespoons chili garlic sauce
- 5 large garlic cloves
- 2 tablespoons honey

Directions

1. Combine pepper with salt in a small bowl & rub the meat with this mixture; ensure all sides are nicely coated. Let sit for 12 to 15 minutes.
2. Next, combine the balsamic vinegar with garlic, chili garlic sauce, olive oil & honey in a non-reactive bowl; mix well.
3. Add in the pork pieces. Cover & let marinate for a couple of hours, turning every now and then.
4. When ready; preheat the grill to 450 F for indirect cooking.
5. Grill the marinated chops over direct heat for 12 to 15 minutes. Turn & grill over indirect heat for an hour.
6. In the meantime, bring the leftover marinade to a boil to use as a sauce. Once the meat is cooked; pour the hot sauce on top. Serve hot & enjoy.

BBQ Pulled Pork

Prep Time: 20 minutes
Cooking Time: 18 hours & 20 minutes
Servings: 16 persons

Ingredients

- 1 bone-in pork shoulder roast (approximately 8 to 10 pounds)
- 2 to 3 tablespoons yellow mustard
- ¼ cup plus 1 tablespoon BBQ Sweet Rub

Directions

1. For indirect smoking; preheat your smoker to 225F.
2. Remove the roast from packaging & wipe all sides down using paper towels, cleaning off any extra liquid or small bone fragments on the exterior.
3. Slather the exterior of the pork shoulder completely with the yellow mustard.
4. Season all sides of the pork roast with the BBQ Sweet Rub; ensure that it's coated liberally.
5. Place the seasoned roast over the smoker in the middle of the grate, fat side up.
6. Close the lid & smoke the pork for 15 to 20 hours.
7. Remove the pork shoulder from smoker & tightly wrap it up in aluminum foil. Let rest for an hour and then do the shredding process.
8. Pull the shoulder apart; discarding any chunks of gristle or fat. Sprinkle the roast with one more tablespoon of the BBQ Rub. Serve immediately & enjoy.

Baby Back Ribs

Prep Time: 3 hours & 20 minutes
Cooking Time: 40 minutes
Servings: 8 persons

Ingredients

- 4 racks baby back pork ribs (2 pounds each)
- 2 tablespoons paprika
- ¼ cup light brown sugar, packed
- 2 tablespoons steak seasoning
- 1 tablespoon apple cider vinegar
- ¼ cup honey
- 1 tablespoon dried oregano
- Vegetable oil, for the grill
- 1 tablespoon ground cumin
- Freshly ground pepper & kosher salt to taste

Directions

1. Turn the ribs bone-side up. Slip a paring knife between the bone and thin membrane to loosen and then, pull the membrane off. Combine brown sugar with steak seasoning, paprika, oregano and cumin in a small-sized mixing bowl; rub this mixture over the ribs; ensure that the pieces are coated nicely. Place on a large-sized baking sheet. Using a plastic wrap; cover & refrigerate for overnight.
2. Preheat a grill over medium high heat & prepare it for indirect grilling.
3. Lightly coat the grates of your grill with oil. Place the ribs on the cooler part of your grill, bone-side down, slightly overlapping if required. Cover & cook for 2 to 2 hours & 15 minutes, until the meat pulls away from the bones and is fork tender, rotating once during the cooking process.
4. Next, combine honey with vinegar & a pinch each of pepper and salt in a small-sized mixing bowl. Transfer the ribs over direct heat; brushing the pieces with the prepared honey mixture; continue grilling for 7 to 10 more minutes, until glazed, uncovered, brushing the pieces one more time with the honey mixture. Transfer to a clean, large cutting board & cut into ribs. Serve immediately & enjoy.

Coca-Cola Ribs

Prep Time: 20 minutes
Cooking Time: 1 hour & 30 minutes
Servings: 6 persons

Ingredients

For The Ribs:

- 1 large onion, quartered
- 2 racks baby back ribs (approximately 4 pounds)
- 1 bottle of Coca-Cola (1.5 liter; ensure it's not a diet version)
- 6 garlic cloves, peeled & smashed
- 1 tablespoon whole black peppercorns
- 2 bay leaves

For The Sauce

- 1 can Coca-Cola (12 ounce; ensure it's not a diet version)
- ⅔ stick butter, unsalted
- 1 cup ketchup
- 2 garlic cloves, minced
- 1 white onion, small, diced
- ¼ cup dark brown sugar
- 1½ tablespoons yellow mustard
- 1 teaspoon Worcestershire sauce
- Freshly ground black pepper & kosher salt, to taste

Directions

1. Fill a large pot with 1.5 liter of Coca-Cola followed by garlic, onion, peppercorns, and bay leaves. Add in the ribs and ensure that the meat is completely submerged, feel free to add some water, if required. Bring the mixture to a boil; once done, decrease the heat to a simmer and continue to cook for an hour, until you can easily pull the meat from the bone, turning the ribs every now and then.

2. In the meantime, prepare the sauce. Over moderate heat in a large heavy saucepan; combine butter with ketchup, onion, garlic, brown sugar, mustard, 12 ounces of Coca-Cola, and Worcestershire sauce; mix well. Bring the mixture to a boil & then, decrease the heat. Let simmer until the sauce is reduced and thickened, for 20 to 25 minutes, stirring often. Season with pepper and salt to taste & let slightly cool. Puree the sauce carefully using a blender.

3. Preheat your grill over high heat.

4. Remove the ribs from pot; pat the pieces dry and then, season with pepper and salt; liberally brush with the prepared sauce. Grill for 7 to 10 minutes, until charred on the outside, turning every now and then. Tent the ribs loosely with aluminum foil & let rest for a couple of minutes then cut into individual ribs. Serve some more sauce on side for dipping. Enjoy.

St. Louis BBQ Ribs

Prep Time: 10 minutes
Cooking Time: 3 hour & 10 minutes
Servings: 8 persons

Ingredients

- 4 pounds St. Louis-style pork ribs, cut into 6-inch sections
- 2 cups barbeque sauce, or to taste

Directions

1. Heat one side of your gas grill to 300F.
2. Fill a small metal container or can with water. Cover with an aluminum foil and make a few slits in the foil with using a sharp parking knife. Place it over the preheated grill.
3. Place ribs on the unheated side of your grill, bone-side up; close the grill & cook for 1 ½ hours; carefully flip the ribs & continue to cook for 1 ½ hours more, until the rib meat shrinks back from the bones.
4. Baste the ribs with some barbeque sauce and place them to the heated side of your grill this time; close the lid & cook for a couple of more minutes. Flip & baste the other side with some barbeque sauce. Close the lid and cook for 2 more minutes. Flip & baste with more of barbeque sauce. Close the lid and cook for 2 more minutes. Serve hot & enjoy.

Texas BBQ Brisket

Prep Time: 6 hours & 10 minutes
Cooking Time: 8 hours & 10 minutes
Servings: 12 persons

Ingredients

- 1 tablespoon chili powder
- 1 beef brisket (approximately 5 to 6 pounds), with a layer of fat, ¼" to ½" thick
- 2 teaspoons sugar
- 1 teaspoon each of ground cumin & freshly ground black pepper
- 1 tablespoon coarse or sea or kosher salt

Directions

1. Rinse the brisket under cold running tap water. Next, using paper towels; blot it completely dry.
2. Combine sugar with cumin, pepper, chili powder, and salt in a medium-sized mixing bowl; gently toss the ingredients until mixed well. Rub the prepared spice mixture on all sides of the brisket. Using a plastic wrap; cover the brisket & place it in a refrigerator for overnight.
3. The next day; preheat a charcoal grill to low heat in advance.
4. When ready, toss 1 ½ cups of the wood chips on the coals (approximately ¾ cup per side). Place the brisket in an aluminum foil pan, fat side up. Place the pan (away from the heat) into the middle of hot grate. Cover the grill & smoke cook the meat for 6 to 7 hours, until tender. Baste the brisket occasionally with the fat & juices that accumulate in the pan. Don't forget to add 10 to 12 pieces of fresh coals to each side after every hour; toss more wood chips on the fresh coals. During the initial 3 hours; every time you refill the coals; add approximately ¾ cup of chips per side.
5. Remove the brisket pan from grill & let rest for several minutes. Transfer the brisket to a clean, large cutting board & thinly slice it across the grain, using an electric knife, sharp knife, or cleaver. Transfer the sliced meat to a large platter; pour the accumulated pan juices on top; serve immediately & enjoy.

Competition Style BBQ Brisket

Prep Time: 30 minutes
Cooking Time: 10 hours & 10 minutes
Servings: 12 persons

Ingredients

- 1 whole packer brisket (12 to 16 pounds)
- ¼ cup butcher BBQ beef injection
- 1 teaspoon onion powder
- ¾ cup black pepper
- 1 teaspoon white pepper
- Coffee rub, as required
- 1 tablespoon beef bouillon
- 2 cup beef broth
- 1 teaspoon garlic powder
- 3 cup water
- 1 cup kosher salt

Directions

1. Preheat your Traeger by setting the temperature to 225 F (lid closed for 12 to 15 minutes).
2. Trim the fat completely off the top of your brisket; leaving approximately ¼" of fat across the bottom.
3. Combine water with onion powder, white pepper, Butcher Beef Injection, beef bouillon and garlic powder in a medium-sized mixing bowl; mix well. Next, using an injector; inject the brisket in a 1" checkerboard pattern across the top of your brisket.
4. Season the brisket with a layer of coffee rub, pepper, and salt.
5. Place the brisket over the preheated grill & smoke for 4 to 4 ½ hours, until the internal temperature of the meat reads 160 F.
6. Wrap the brisket in a double layer of heavy-duty aluminum foil. Pour approximately 2 cups of the beef broth into the foil packet with the brisket & place it over the grill again.
7. Turn grill temperature up to 250F & cook until internal temperature of the meat reads 204 F, for 4 to 4 ½ more hours. Once done; immediately pull the meat off the grill & wrap it in a kitchen towel.
8. Let rest on the counter for an hour, wrapped and then, slice it against the grain. Serve and enjoy.

Apricot Chili Glazed BBQ Chicken

Prep Time: 20 minutes
Cooking Time: 40 minutes
Servings: 12 persons

Ingredients

- ½ cup apricots, dried, chopped
- 6 skinless, boneless chicken breasts
- ½ teaspoon each of pepper & red pepper flakes
- 2 tablespoons spicy brown mustard
- ⅔ cup plus 4 tablespoons chicken broth
- 2 tablespoons soy sauce
- ¾ cup apricot preserves
- 2 teaspoon lemon zest, fresh
- ¼ teaspoon each of garlic powder & salt

Directions

1. Create two thinner pieces out of each chicken's breast by cutting it horizontally into half. Cover & refrigerate until ready to cook.
2. Combine 4 tablespoons of the broth with apricots & apricot preserves, in a medium-sized mixing bowl; mix well. Stir in the soy sauce, mustard, garlic powder, pepper flakes, lemon zest, pepper, and salt.
3. Let rest at room temperature while you heat your grill.
4. Heat your grill to 375 F, over medium high heat. For nice grill marks; place the chicken over grill diagonally at a 45-degree angle. Let cook for 5 minutes and then, rotate it to 90 degrees & continue to cook for 2 to 3 more minutes.
5. Carefully flip the chicken pieces & repeat this cooking step on the other side as well.
6. Once done, generously baste the chicken with the prepared apricot sauce. Carefully flip & baste the other side as well; cook for 1 to 2 minutes, until a meat thermometer reads an internal temperature of 165 F; ensure that you don't overcook the chicken.
7. Remove the chicken from grill & cover it with aluminum foil. Let rest for 8 to 10 minutes before serving.
8. For Sauce: Over moderate heat in a small-sized saucepan; heat ⅔ cup of chicken broth with the leftover apricot sauce. Stir & let simmer until thickened. Once done; pour over the grilled chicken.

Caribbean BBQ Chicken

Prep Time: 10 minutes
Cooking Time: 30 minutes
Servings: 5 persons

Ingredients

- ½ teaspoon thyme leaves, dried
- 1 broiler-fryer chicken (approximately 3 pounds), cut up
- ½ teaspoon each of black pepper & cayenne (ground red pepper)
- 1 teaspoon each of onion powder & garlic powder
- ½ cup Brown Sugar & Hickory Barbecue Sauce
- 2 tablespoons lime juice, fresh
- ½ teaspoon ground cinnamon

Directions

1. Preheat your grill over medium heat in advance. Trim & discard any excess fat from the chicken.
2. Combine the seasonings in a small-sized mixing bowl until blended well; stir in the lime juice until you get paste like consistency. Rub this evenly over the chicken pieces.
3. Place the coated chicken on the grill, skin-side up; cover with a lid & grill for 25 minutes, turning & brushing with approximately ¼ cup of the barbecue sauce after ever 12 to 15 minutes. Turn the chicken over; brush with the leftover barbecue sauce. Continue to grill until the chicken is cooked through, for 5 more minutes.

Sweet Bourbon BBQ Chicken

Prep Time: 10 minutes
Cooking Time: 20 minutes
Servings: 4 persons

Ingredients

- Chicken boneless, bone in, thighs or breasts
- ½ to 1 tablespoon Bourbon or Whisky
- 2 tablespoon honey
- ½ cup barbecue sauce
- Pepper & salt to taste

Directions

1. Pat the chicken dry & trim, as required.
2. Season with pepper and salt to taste.
3. Combine the barbecue sauce with Whiskey/Bourbon and honey; give the ingredients a good stir until completely blended and smooth.
4. Lightly oil the grill grate and heat it to over medium high heat. When hot, carefully place the coated chicken over the hot grill & cook until done, flipping the pieces once.
5. When placing the chicken pieces over the hot grill ensure that you don't brush the face downside with the sauce; simply brush the topside. Brush the other side only after flipping it; cook until done.
6. Remove from the grill & brush the chicken with more sauce on both sides; serve immediately & enjoy.

BBQ Jamaican Jerk Chicken

Prep Time: 30 minutes
Cooking Time: 9 hours & 10 minutes
Servings: 8 persons

Ingredients

- 1 tablespoon pepper, coarsely ground
- 2 whole chickens (3 ½ to 4 pounds), quartered
- 1 onion, medium, coarsely chopped
- 3 scallions, medium, chopped
- 1 tablespoon allspice berries, coarsely ground
- 2 Scotch bonnet chiles, chopped
- 1 tablespoon five-spice powder
- 1 teaspoon thyme, dried & crumbled
- 2 garlic cloves, chopped
- 1 teaspoon nutmeg, freshly grated
- ½ cup soy sauce
- 1 tablespoon vegetable oil
- 1 teaspoon salt

Directions

1. Combine onion with five-spice powder, chiles, scallions, thyme, garlic, allspice, nutmeg, pepper, and salt in a food processor; process on high speed until you get coarse paste like consistency. With the machine still on; add in the oil and soy sauce in a slow and steady stream. Pour the prepared marinade into a large, shallow dish; add in the chicken pieces; turning them several times until nicely coated. Cover & refrigerate for overnight. When ready to cook; bring the chicken to room temperature.
2. Light a grill; grill the chicken over medium-hot fire for 35 to 40 minutes, until cooked through & browned well, turning every now and then. (For a smokier flavor; cover the grill.) Transfer the cooked chicken to a large platter; serve immediately & enjoy.

Desserts

Spiced grilled pineapple with maple brittle

Prep Time: 10 minutes
Cooking Time: 20 minutes
Servings: 4 persons

Ingredients

- A pinch each of ground ginger & mixed spice
- 2 limes, juice & zest, fresh
- 1 medium ripe pineapple
- Vegetable oil , for grilling
- 3 tablespoons maple syrup
- A small handful of mint leaves or Thai basil and frozen yogurt or thick Greek yogurt, to serve

For The Brittle
- 100g caster sugar
- 25g maple syrup
- 100g butter
- ½ teaspoon sea salt flakes
- 50g sesame seeds

Directions

1. For Brittle: Line a large, heavy baking tray with parchment paper. Next, over moderate heat in a heavy-based saucepan; add sugar with maple syrup, butter & 25ml of water; giving the ingredients a good stir and cook for 12 to 15 minutes, until the sugar has melted and dark golden brown. Stir in the sea salt flakes and sesame seeds; briefly stir then, pour the prepared mixture over the lined tray; set aside to cool & harden.

2. Combine the lime juice with most of the lime zest, ground ginger, maple syrup and mixed spice. Top & tail the pineapple, cut away any black marks & the skin from the flesh, then cut into 1cm slices. Toss with the lime-maple mix; let rest for 30 minutes.

3. Wait until the embers are low on a barbecue. Oil the grill bars lightly & grill the pineapple until turn golden & charred lightly, for a minute or two per side. Cut into bite-sized shards and then, transfer to a large platter while you cook the remaining pineapple.

4. Finely slice the larger mint leaves or basil & keep the smaller leaves whole. Bash the brittle into pieces; serve scattered on top of the charred pineapple with the herbs & a drizzle of the prepared marinade. Scatter the leftover lime zest on top of the frozen yogurt or yogurt; serve on the side & enjoy.

BBQ Banana Splits

Prep Time: 10 minutes
Cooking Time: 20 minutes
Servings: 4 persons

Ingredients

- 4 ripe bananas, splits
- 8 teaspoons butter, unsalted, cut into small-sized pieces
- 3 cups vanilla ice cream
- 4 teaspoons vanilla or rum extract, coconut extract, or lemon extract or even brandy
- 8 teaspoons chocolate syrup
- 4 tablespoons light brown sugar
- ¼ cup pecans, toasted; any of your favorite

Directions

1. Preheat your grill over low. Make & incision lengthwise on the side of each banana; leaving approximately 1" uncut at both ends & the skin intact. Spread the cut open & place approximately 2 teaspoons of butter pieces followed by 1 teaspoon of vanilla & 1 tablespoon of brown sugar.
2. Cover & grill for 8 to 10 minutes, until bananas are heated through, and the butter mixture has completely melted. Move the bananas to 4 separate sundae dishes, flipping the bananas carefully over & pouring the sauce into the bottom of each dish.
3. Peel the skins off & top each with an equal quantity of ice cream; add in the warm chocolate sauce & nuts. Serve immediately & enjoy.

S'mores Dip

Prep Time: 10 minutes
Cooking Time: 10 minutes
Servings: 12 persons

Ingredients

- 3 cups mini marshmallows
- 12 ounces small peanut butter cups
- graham crackers

Directions

1. Line a 10" foil pie pan with the peanut butter cups and then, top with the marshmallows. Broil for 12 to 15 seconds, until golden. Cover & grill over low heat for 3 to 5 minutes, until chocolate is melted. Serve with some graham crackers for dipping. Enjoy.

Grilled Peaches with Balsamic Glaze

Prep Time: 10 minutes
Cooking Time: 30 minutes
Servings: 4 persons

Ingredients

- 4 ripe peaches, halved & pitted
- 1 tablespoon brown sugar
- ½ cup balsamic vinegar
- 1 teaspoon almond extract
- Vegetable oil cooking spray, butter-flavored, to taste
- 1 tablespoon lemon juice, fresh
- Fresh mint sprigs (to garnish)

Directions

1. Preheat a gas grill over medium-high heat in advance. Coat the peach halves with some cooking spray.
2. Place the peaches over the hot grill, cut side down & grill until grill marks start to appear & peaches are softened slightly, for 3 to 5 minutes per side.
3. In the meantime, prepare the glaze. Over medium-high heat in a small saucepan; bring vinegar to a boil; continue to cook until it looks thick and is decreased by half.
4. Add almond extract, lemon juice & sugar.
5. Remove the peaches from grill & place on a dessert dish, cut side up. Drizzle with the balsamic glaze & garnish with a fresh sprig of mint.

BBQ Blueberry-Rhubarb Crumble

Prep Time: 20 minutes
Cooking Time: 20 minutes
Servings: 6 persons

Ingredients

- ¼ teaspoon ground cinnamon
- 3 cups blueberries, fresh or frozen
- ½ cup granulated sugar
- 2 cups diced rhubarb, fresh or frozen
- ½ cup quick cooking rolled oats
- 2 tablespoons all-purpose flour
- ¼ cup all-purpose flour
- ½ cup brown sugar, packed
- ¼ teaspoon ground nutmeg
- Whipped cream, optional
- ¼ cup margarine or butter

Directions

1. Over moderate heat in a medium-sized saucepan; combine blueberries with the granulated sugar, rhubarb & 2 tablespoons of flour. Cook & stir the ingredients for a couple of minutes, until bubbly and thickened. Transfer the fruit mixture into an 8x8x2" metal baking pan; set aside until ready to use.
2. For Topping: Combine the oats with ¼ cup flour, brown sugar, cinnamon, and nutmeg in a medium-sized mixing bowl. Cut in the margarine or butter until you get coarse crumbs like consistency. Sprinkle the prepared topping on top of the fruit mixture. Tightly cover the pan with aluminum foil.
3. Grill until the topping is just set, for 20 to 25 minutes. Serve warm with the optional whipped cream. Enjoy.

BBQ Cake & Berry Campfire Cobbler

Prep Time: 20 minutes
Cooking Time: 40 minutes
Servings: 6 persons

Ingredients

- 6 peaches, chopped
- 2 tablespoons cornstarch
- 1 cup blueberries
- 2 cups raspberries
- 1 cup strawberries, chopped
- 2 teaspoons ground cinnamon
- ¼ cup plus 2 tablespoons sugar, divided
- 2 ⅓ cup Bisquick Mix
- A pinch of kosher salt
- ½ cup milk

Directions

1. Combine the fruit with ¼ cup of sugar, cinnamon, cornstarch & salt in a large resealable plastic bag. Tightly seal the bag & shake until fruit is coated evenly.
2. Combine Bisquick with milk in a separate resealable plastic bag, large-sized. Seal & mix until combined completely; kneading with your hands.
3. Coat a large-sized cast-iron skillet with butter and then, add the fruit mixture; top with the prepared Bisquick topping. Sprinkle with the leftover sugar.
4. Cover with aluminum foil & cook over a campfire for 50 minutes, until fruit is warm & bubbly and biscuits are no longer doughy.
5. Let cool for 20 minutes; serve and enjoy.

BBQ Banana Butter pecan Kabobs

Prep Time: 15 minutes
Cooking Time: 25 minutes
Servings: 8 persons

Ingredients

- ½ teaspoon vanilla extract
- 1 loaf pound cake (approximately 10 ¾ ounces), frozen, thawed & cubed
- ¼ cup melted butter
- 2 bananas, large, cut into 1" slices
- ⅛ teaspoon ground cinnamon
- 2 tablespoons brown sugar
- ½ cup butterscotch ice cream topping
- 4 cups pecan butter ice cream
- ½ cup chopped pecans, toasted

Directions

1. Thread bananas and cake alternately on four soaked wooden or metal skewers. Combine butter with vanilla, brown sugar & cinnamon in a small-sized mixing bowl; brush this mixture over the kabobs.
2. Place the kabobs on a lightly greased grill rack. Cover & grill the kabobs over medium heat until browned, for 3 to 4 minutes, turning them once.
3. Serve with ice cream; topped with the butterscotch. Sprinkle with the pecans. Enjoy.

Original Campfire S'mores

Prep Time: 10 minutes
Cooking Time: 10 minutes
Servings: 4 persons

Ingredients

- 4 Jet-Puffed Marshmallow's
- ½ cup Baker's Chocolate Chunks, Semi-Sweet
- 4 graham crackers, broken in half (approximately 8 squares)

Directions

1. Preheat your grill over medium heat in advance.
2. Fill the graham squares with leftover ingredients to prepare 4 smores; wrap each S'more in a heavy-duty foil.
3. Grill until marshmallows are completely melted, for 3 to 5 minutes.

Grilled Cranberry Pear Crumble

Prep Time: 20 minutes
Cooking Time: 30 minutes
Servings: 6 persons

Ingredients

- 3 pears, medium, ripe, sliced
- ¼ teaspoon ground cinnamon
- 2 tablespoons all-purpose flour
- ½ cup cranberries, dried
- 1 tablespoon butter
- ¼ cup sugar

For Topping:
- 2 tablespoons melted butter
- 1 cup granola without raisins
- ¼ teaspoon ground cinnamon

Directions

1. Toss the cranberries and pears with flour, sugar & cinnamon. Place 1 tablespoon of butter in a 9" cast-iron skillet. Place it over the grill rack on medium heat until the butter is completely melted. Stir in the fruit; grill, for 15 to 20 minutes, until pears are tender, covered, stirring every now and then.
2. For topping: Combine the melted butter with cinnamon; toss with the granola. Sprinkle on top of the pears. Grill for 5 more minutes, covered. Serve warm and enjoy.

BBQ Blackout Peach Bread Pudding

Prep Time: 30 minutes
Cooking Time: 20 minutes
Servings: 6 persons

Ingredients

- 4 large egg yolks
- ¼ cup mascarpone cheese
- 1 cup whole milk
- 2 medium peaches, halved & pitted
- ½ teaspoon ground cinnamon
- 1 tablespoon butter, melted
- 4 potato dinner rolls, halved
- ½ cup caramel sundae syrup
- 2 tablespoons brown sugar
- Sweetened whipped cream, optional
- ⅓ cup sugar

Directions

1. Whisk egg yolks with mascarpone cheese, sugar, whole milk & ground cinnamon until blended well in a small-sized mixing bowl; refrigerate until ready to use.
2. Brush the peaches with melted butter. Cover & grill on a lightly oiled rack for 5 to 6 minutes, until browned lightly, over medium heat, turning once. Grill the rolls for 2 to 3 more minutes, until browned lightly, uncovered, turning once. Let slightly cool; cut the rolls and peaches into ¾" cubes.
3. Combine peaches with brown sugar in a large bowl and then, stir in the bread cubes. Spoon into 12 well-greased, disposable aluminum muffin cups. Pour the muffin cups with the prepared egg mixture.
4. Cover & grill over indirect high heat for 12 to 15 minutes. Let cool in the pan for a couple of minutes before removing. Serve with caramel syrup and whipped cream. Enjoy.

Sign-up Now
and Be Notified of New Books

Website: readbooks.today

Printed in Great Britain
by Amazon

42685324R00040